the Little Penguin™
cookbook

Twenty-six recipes and wine pairings from the kitchen of
Sally James

Sally James
the Little Penguin Cookbook
First Edition

ISBN: 0-9773983-0-7

Printed in the United States of America
Photography: Gregory Ross of Ross Studios, Napa CA
Food and Prop Styling: Sally James
Food stylist assistant: Namon File
Project Editor: Karina Reiswig
Production Editor: Andrea Martin
Edited by Joann Ferguson and Karina Reiswig
Art Direction and Graphic Design: Christopher Hayes
Printing: Imperial— A Visual Communication Company, Milwaukee, WI
Distributed by the Little Penguin Wines

Seafood supplied by Osprey Seafoods, San Francisco

Table Setting Acknowledgements:
Page 18: Flowerpot by Bison, Australia
Page 40: Fused Glass Plates by Erika Von Zoog, Studio 113
Page 50: Plates by Bison, Australia
Page 66: Fused Glass Plates by Erika Von Zoog, Studio 113

Any items not credited are privately owned

contents

"Clearly, the pleasures wines afford are transitory — but so are those of the ballet, or of a musical performance. Wine is inspiring and adds greatly to the joy of living."

— Napoleon Bonaparte

When I was asked to write the Little Penguin Cookbook, I jumped with delight. Create recipes to be enjoyed with a glass of great wine? Definitely! That's my passion! Not only do I firmly believe that food and wine, together, bring us one of life's greatest pleasures, but the Little Penguin is about enjoying each day to its fullest; having fun and experiencing good food and wine— but not too seriously. That's just the way I believe cooking should be.

There will always be the place for those special occasions where we stare with awe at wondrous creations before us and savor each sip of an exclusive wine slowly allowing it to linger endlessly on our tongues to appreciate its complexity. But just as you don't need to spend a fortune to enjoy an immensely enjoyable fine wine, neither should you have to spend hours cooking or hunting for ingredients to create a stunning looking and delicious meal.

My recipes are designed to indulge all the senses— smell, sight, touch (yes, cooking and eating with your hands is acceptable— ask the Italians) and, of course, taste. But more importantly, they are designed with simplicity to allow the preparer time to enjoy the occasion of eating and sipping great wine with family and friends. I also believe that dishes prepared with simplicity and focus, make a much better companion to wine.

You'll find that a lot of my recipes contain wine, which I often cook with. Wine adds a wonderful dimension and depth to many dishes, but don't feel bound to stick with my choices. As with the Little Penguin philosophy, there are no rules. Try with the wines you prefer, and, most importantly, play with my recipes to your heart's content. There's nothing better than experimenting with recipes using all of those senses and finding the inner cook in you!

Bon Apetit! And may you always delight in the simple joy of preparing and sharing a meal.

—Sally James, WineRoads.com

white shiraz

sweet corn soup with crab salsa

Serves 4-6

Warm weather beckons fresh flavors and quick meals. I dressed up this soup by adding a fresh crab salsa with a dash of chili— the perfect combination for the sweet corn and a glass of the Little Penguin White Shiraz.

SWEET CORN SOUP
1 tablespoon olive oil
2 green onions, chopped
2 teaspoons grated ginger
Fresh kernels from 5 ears corn
1 ½ cups chicken stock
1 cup buttermilk or low-fat milk
white pepper, sea salt and lemon juice
   to taste

CRAB SALSA
¾ cup fresh crab meat
2 Roma tomatoes, seeded and diced
¼ cup chopped cilantro
juice and zest of ½ lemon
dash chili sauce or Tabasco (optional)

Combine all the salsa ingredients and refrigerate until ready to use.

To make the soup, heat oil in a large saucepan, add green onions and ginger and sauté for 1-2 minutes or until starting to soften. Set aside half a cup of the corn and add the remainder to the pan. Cook, stirring for 1 minute then add chicken stock. Bring to boil and simmer 4-5 minutes. Using an immersion blender or blender, process the soup until smooth. Return to the pan, add the reserved corn and buttermilk and season to taste. Reheat and serve with a spoon of the crab salsa.

While the White Shiraz follows the whole summery theme of this dish with its tangy fresh zip, I'd also try with the Little Penguin Pinot Noir or Merlot - the contrast of the rich fruit and earthy tones of the wine and the sweetness of the corn is really quite defiantly delicious!

This dish is the perfect simple, yet delectable, summer dish. The fish can be prepared a few hours ahead of time, making it quick to assemble. Just remember, the longer it marinates, the more it "cooks" in the lime juice.

ceviche in endive cups

Makes 14-16 cups

1 pound very fresh fish, try snapper, halibut, swordfish, tuna or preferred fish, skin and bones removed

1 small red jalapeno pepper, finely diced

2 Roma tomatoes, seeded and finely diced

½ small red onion, finely diced

2 tablespoons chopped chives

¼ cup chopped cilantro

juice of 2 limes

3 heads endive, large leaves separated

Chop the seafood into small even pieces, discarding any dark flesh. Place in a non-reactive bowl. Add the remaining ceviche ingredients and mix well. Cover with plastic and refrigerate for 2-3 hours or until ready to serve. To serve, trim the ends from the endive leaves and place a spoon of the ceviche in each endive cup. Serve straight away with a chilled glass of the Little Penguin White Shiraz or Chardonnay.

five spice pork, fig & fresh herb salad

Serves 4

1 – 1 ½ pound pork loin or chops
olive oil, for cooking

MARINADE
2 tablespoons honey, softened
2 tablespoons soy sauce
2 teaspoons Chinese 5 Spice
1 tablespoon red wine vinegar

SALAD
juice of ½ lemon
2 tablespoons olive oil
½ bulb fennel (white part) finely sliced
½ bunch cilantro, roughly chopped
½ bunch basil, leaves torn
½ bunch mint, leaves torn
8 fresh figs, quartered

Combine the honey, soy, Chinese 5 spice and vinegar in a flat-based casserole or dish and mix well. Place the pork loin in the marinade and turn to cover the pork completely with the mixture. Cover and refrigerate for 1 hour or overnight.

Preheat oven to 350°F. Remove pork from marinade allowing excess to drip off. Reserve marinade. Heat an ovenproof pan over medium heat and add enough oil to coat the base. Cook the pork for 2-3 minutes on all sides or until browned. Brush generously with extra marinade, cover loosely with foil and place in the oven. Roast for 10-12 minutes or until cooked as desired. For the moistest cut, don't overcook the pork. It's OK to still be pale pink inside. Remove from oven and allow to rest for 10 minutes or chill completely before slicing.

Whisk the lemon and olive oil together. Place the fennel and herbs in a large bowl and add the dressing. Toss well to combine. Place the herb salad on a platter and arrange the sliced pork over the top. Scatter the figs around the dish and serve with a loaf of crusty bread.

The flavors of Chinese 5 Spice draw the pork and the Little Penguin White Shiraz together like a marriage. But the richness of the pork, the saltiness of the soy and the sweetness of the honey and figs make this dish equally at home with the Little Penguin Chardonnay, Shiraz or Pinot Noir.

It seemed appropriate at some stage in this book to bring the juice and the fruit together. the Little Penguin White Shiraz, being slightly sweet, yet having a delicious berry nose and palate makes a superb base for a syrup to engulf plump grapes.

marinated grape parfaits

Serves 4-6

2 cups the Little Penguin White Shiraz
⅓ cup sugar, or to taste
3 cups mixed seedless grapes
1 cup light cream cheese
½ cup flavored yogurt

Place the wine and sugar in a saucepan and bring to the boil. Reduce heat and simmer until sugar has dissolved and mixture has thickened slightly. Taste and adjust sweetness if desired. Place the grapes in a bowl and pour over wine syrup. Cover and refrigerate until chilled. Using an electric mixer, beat together the cream cheese, yogurt and sugar if desired. Refrigerate until ready to assemble parfaits.

To serve, place some grapes with a little wine syrup in the bottom of glasses. Spoon over some of the crème mixture. Repeat as many times as the glass allows ending with the crème. Drizzle over a little of the syrup and serve straight away.

chardonnay

Intense Asian flavors are often hard to find a good wine match for, as they tend to leave your mouth dry. So, the nice rounded the Little Penguin Chardonnay or Shiraz would be my pick to compliment the satay, yet not overpower the chicken.

satay chicken skewers

Makes 8-10 skewers

1 pound skinless chicken breast fillets
3 green onions

PAPAYA RELISH
½ papaya, flesh mashed
juice of ½ lime
2 tablespoons finely chopped cilantro
pinch brown sugar

SATAY SAUCE
¼ cup fresh peanut butter
2 teaspoons soy sauce
1 teaspoon lemon juice
1-2 teaspoons sugar
1 clove garlic, crushed
1 teaspoon sweet chili sauce, or to taste

Remove any excess fat from chicken and cut into 1-inch cubes. Peel green onions and cut, diagonally, into 1-inch pieces. Combine the satay sauce ingredients in a bowl and mix to a smooth paste. Add a little water if necessary to make a thick sauce consistency. Add the chicken, stir well, cover and refrigerate for 30 minutes to an hour.

Combine the papaya relish ingredients and mix well. Refrigerate until ready to serve. Soak 10 bamboo skewers in cold water for 20 minutes to prevent burning. Remove chicken from marinade, brushing off excess, and thread onto skewers alternately with the green onions. Heat a barbecue or grill to high and cook chicken, turning, for 6-8 minutes or until chicken is cooked through. Serve with the papaya relish for dipping.

oven-roasted fish fingers with tartar sauce

Serves 4-6

Deep frying can be a pain and sometimes all that oil hanging around isn't that desirable (let the chefs do that for you when you go out). Here's a much easier version that's quicker and simpler to make, and, by using the oat or corn flakes, ensures that wonderful crunch and crispness.

1 ¼ pound firm white fish fillets, skin and bones removed, for example, halibut, sturgeon, mahi mahi, bass

1 cup oat or corn flakes

1 cup panko or dry breadcrumbs

¼ cup sesame seeds

1 tablespoon chopped oregano or parsley

2 eggs, lightly beaten

2 tablespoons buttermilk

½ cup seasoned flour

TARTAR SAUCE

⅓ cup plain yogurt

2 tablespoons mayonnaise

1 tablespoon tomato paste

2 tablespoons finely diced dill pickles or capers

juice of ½ lemon

Preheat oven to 375°F. Line an oven tray with parchment paper. Using a sharp knife, cut the fish fillets into large strips, or desired sized pieces. Place the oat flakes, panko, sesame seeds and oregano in a food processor and process until mixture looks like coarse breadcrumbs. Spread mixture out on a flat dish. Whisk together the egg and buttermilk and place in a separate bowl. Place the flour in a zip lock bag, add the fish and shake well to coat all sides. Remove the fish and shake off excess flour. Dip into egg mixture, then roll fillets in the crumb mixture, pressing down well to coat. Place on lined tray.

Bake for 10-15 minutes or until crisp and golden. The cooking time will vary depending on type of fish. To test, insert a thin sharp knife into the edge of the fish and gently press. The fish should separate easily, but still be plump and moist inside.

While the fish is cooking combine the tartar ingredients in a bowl and mix well. Serve the fish with the tartar sauce and a green salad.

There are so many wonderful yet simple ways to make gourmet burgers– try fish, seafood, lamb or pork, mixed with nuts, fresh herbs and spices or even a surprise element hidden inside, like some rich, soft cheese - a sure way to bring the food to the wine.

fresh tuna burgers with mango salsa

Makes 6 burgers

BURGERS

1 ¾ pound fresh sushi grade tuna, cut into large pieces

1 egg

2 green onions, finely chopped

¼ cup finely chopped parsley

2 tablespoons pine nuts

sea salt and cracked pepper, to taste

½ cup polenta or coarse cornmeal

MANGO SALSA

1 mango, diced

1 Roma tomato, seeded and diced

½ cup diced English or Persian cucumber

¼ cup finely diced red onion

2 tablespoons chopped cilantro

juice of 1 lime

2 tablespoons plain yogurt

Place tuna in a food processor. Using the pulse switch, process on and off just to coarsely grind. If you don't have a food processor, cut the tuna into as fine a dice as possible. Transfer to a bowl and, using hands, mix in the egg, green onions, parsley, pine nuts, salt and pepper. Shape into burgers. Spread the polenta on a plate. Press the burgers onto the polenta to coat both sides. Cover with plastic and refrigerate for thirty minutes.

Combine the ingredients for the mango salsa and refrigerate until ready to use. (Both the burgers and salsa can be made a few hours ahead.) Heat a grill or heavy based fry pan over a medium high heat and add enough oil to coat pan. Cook burgers for 3-4 minutes, flip over and continue cooking for 2-3 minutes or until browned. The tuna should still be pink and moist inside. When the burgers are nearly cooked, lightly grill the cut side of the rolls. To serve, place a mound of leaves on the warm rolls. Top with the burger and spoon over the mango salsa.

insalata tricolor with pears and goat cheese

Serves 6

1 head radicchio lettuce, leaves separated

2 heads endive, leaves separated

1 bunch arugula

2 tablespoons extra virgin olive oil

1 tablespoon lemon juice

salt and freshly ground pepper, to taste

2 pears, diced (try a variety of colors for interest)

⅓ cup finely sliced fennel

¼ cup soft goat cheese (chevre)

1 tablespoon buttermilk

1 tablespoon olive oil

1 tablespoon red wine vinegar

CARAMELIZED PECANS

1 tablespoon Tamari or soy sauce

¼ cup pecans

1 tablespoon brown sugar

Preheat oven to 350°F. To make caramelized pecans, place the nuts in a bag and toss with the Tamari or soy. Add the sugar and toss to coat. Place nuts on a lined baking tray and bake for 5-7 minutes or until toasted. When cool, crumble pecans and set aside.

Place the lettuce leaves in a bowl. Whisk together oil and lemon juice, season to taste, and toss through the leaves. Place the pears and fennel in a separate bowl. Beat together cheese, buttermilk, oil and vinegar and toss through the pears and fennel. To serve, arrange the leaves around a platter and make a mound of the pear mixture in the center. Scatter with the pecans and serve with a loaf of Pugliese or Italian bread and olive oil, for dipping.

A trick to making a salad more wine-friendly is to add ingredients we know are great with wine. In this recipe, I've chosen goat cheese and pecans, but feel free to add your own wine-welcoming ingredients such as shaved proscuitto, parmesan, blueberries or other fanciful ingredient.

merlot

Choose zucchini that are small, dark green and firm for the best flavor. For variety, you may like to try a mixture of green and yellow zucchini or substituting other summer squash. For a non-vegetarian option, add cooked tuna, prawns or chicken.

zucchini and peanut pasta salad

Serves 4-6

12 ounces short pasta such as penne, shells or large macaroni

3 zucchini, thickly sliced

3 Roma tomatoes, diced or 1 cup halved cherry tomatoes

⅓ cup unsalted dry roasted peanuts

HERB VINAIGRETTE

2 tablespoons extra virgin olive oil

1 tablespoon lemon juice

1 tablespoon white wine vinegar

1 teaspoon Dijon mustard

1 green onion, finely chopped

2 tablespoons chopped parsley or basil

Whisk together the vinaigrette ingredients and set aside. Cook pasta according to directions on packet, drain and place in a large bowl. Toss with dressing. Blanch the zucchini for 1-2 minutes or until just starting to soften. Pour into a sieve and rinse well with cold water to stop further cooking. Add to the pasta with the tomatoes and peanuts and toss well. Serve warm or refrigerate to serve chilled.

Most people use vodka to spruce up a Gazpacho, but I found that the Little Penguin Merlot added a wonderful dimension and roundness to the dish. Experiment yourself to find your own designer blend. For a more flavorful soup, take the time to allow the flavors to develop overnight.

gazpacho and merlot shooters

Serves 4-6

3 tomatoes, diced (try heirloom or other
   full flavored seasonal tomatoes)
1 Persian or ½ English cucumber, diced
1 yellow or green pepper, diced
2 tablespoons tomato paste
1 cup tomato juice
1 tablespoon lemon juice

1 tablespoon red wine vinegar
¼ cup roughly chopped parsley
salt and freshly ground pepper, to taste
2 tablespoons extra virgin olive oil
¼ cup the Little Penguin Merlot,
   or to taste

Place all the ingredients except the Merlot in a blender and puree until smooth. Chill for an hour or overnight. For a smoother soup, strain mixture through a sieve. Just before serving, add the wine and stir well. Taste and adjust seasoning or add more wine as desired. Serve in shooter glasses.

grilled asparagus and prosciutto bruschetta

Serves 6-8

This is my favorite food to serve for a relaxing lunch. It's so easy to prepare, and the mixture of saltiness from the prosciutto and capers, creamy tartness of the cheese, aromas of the herbs and grassiness of the asparagus make it a virtual playground for a wine pairing.

8-10 large basil leaves

1 sprig parsley, chopped

½ cup extra virgin olive oil

16 stalks fresh asparagus, trimmed

6-8 thick slices Italian bread or ciabatta

1 clove garlic, halved

4 tablespoons soft goat cheese

6-8 slices Prosciutto, trimmed

1 tablespoon capers

cracked pepper to taste

Bring a pot of water to boil, add basil leaves and blanch for 10 seconds. Remove from water and dry well in a paper towel. Place in a blender with the parsley and process, scraping down edges until finely chopped. With the motor running, add the oil gradually in a steady stream. Process until mixture is smooth. Strain into a bottle or jar and set aside.

Brush the asparagus with some of the basil oil. Heat a grill or sauté pan and cook the asparagus for 1-2 minutes, turning, until just tender. Keep warm. Place the bread on the grill or panini maker and cook until browned. Rub with the garlic clove.

To serve, spread the hot bread with the goat cheese and top with the prosciutto. Lay 2 spears asparagus on the prosciutto, drizzle with the basil oil and garnish with a few capers. Serve while warm.

I don't think I've ever had more fun creating a recipe than this one. The idea was to pick a few of the characteristics of the Little Penguin Merlot, and bring them to life. So I chose the berry and chocolate notes, and just had to finish it with a velvety dollop of Crème Fraîche, to round it all out.

blueberry merlot frappé with crème fraîche

Makes 2 (after all, it's such a seductive dish!)

½ cup frozen blueberries
1 tablespoon sugar, or to taste
¼-½ cup the Little Penguin Merlot
2 tablespoons Crème Fraîche
2-inch piece dark chocolate cut into
   shards

Place the frozen blueberries and sugar in a blender and puree until smooth. Gradually add the Merlot until desired consistency. Taste and add more sugar if desired. (You can refreeze in ice cubes at this stage, if desired. Just before serving, place cubes in blender and purée.)

To serve, spoon frappe into wine glasses, top with a spoon of Crème Fraîche and the chocolate shards. Serve straight away.

shiraz

tomato ricotta tarts with pine nut pastry

Makes 4 individual tarts

Nuts are healthy and also very wine-friendly foods. Making this pastry from nuts adds an earthy character to the tarts and is easy to prepare. You can also try this recipe with hazelnuts, macadamias or roasted almonds. In a hurry? Just use frozen pastry dough.

PINE NUT PASTRY
¾ cup pine nuts
1 ½ cups plain flour
3 tablespoons extra virgin olive oil
⅓-½ cup chilled skim milk

FILLING
1 cup fresh ricotta cheese
16-20 cherry tomatoes, halved
freshly ground pepper to taste

To make the tart shell, preheat oven to 375° F. Place pine nuts and flour in a food processor and process until most of nuts are ground. With the motor running, add the oil and then gradually pour in enough skim milk until mixture comes together. Take care not to overmix. Transfer to a floured board and knead gently to a smooth dough.

Roll out pastry on a floured board to a large square, about 14 -16 inches. Trim edges and cut into 4 pieces. Brush edges with water. Fold in about 1/2-inch along each edge and then again to form a rim. Pinch corners and sides to seal rim into place. Lift the tart shells onto a lined baking tray and prick the base of each square a few times with a fork. Bake for 12-15 minutes or until just starting to brown.

Allow to cool slightly on a wire rack. Spread the ricotta cheese evenly over the base of the tart. Place cherry tomatoes over the top and season to taste with pepper. Bake for 7-8 minutes or until tomatoes just start to soften. Serve hot or cold.

The dark sweet fruit of the Shiraz accentuates the flavor of the plums and makes this a perfect pairing. This relish is also delicious with grilled fish, pork, meats or just spread cold on bread. It can be stored for up to 3 days in a sealed container in the refrigerator.

char-grilled chicken with plum relish

Serves 4

4 chicken breast fillets
olive oil, for cooking

RELISH
½ red onion, diced
2 teaspoons olive oil
2 tablespoons brown sugar
1 cup diced plums

RELISH (cont.)
2 tablespoons balsamic or red wine vinegar
1 tablespoon lemon juice
½ cup the Little Penguin Shiraz

To make relish, cook diced onion in oil over a medium heat until soft. Add the sugar and plums and cook, stirring for 2-3 minutes. Add the remaining ingredients. Reduce heat and simmer for 10 -15 minutes or until syrupy.

Preheat oven to 350° F. Brush the chicken with oil and grill over medium heat for 2-3 minutes each side until golden brown. Transfer to oven and cook for 10-15 minutes or until cooked through but still plump and moist. To test, pierce with a sharp knife and the juices should run clear. Slice the chicken thickly and spoon over the relish.

thai-cured lamb and noodle salad

Some food and wine combinations are just meant to be– like lamb and Shiraz. Especially when they're both from Australia where the lamb is milder, leaner and sweeter. You may also like to try with the Little Penguin Pinot Noir, or Chardonnay to round out the zest of the curry paste.

Serves 4

1 pound lamb fillet or loin
1-2 tablespoons peanut or canola oil,
  for cooking

DRESSING
juice of ½ lime
1 teaspoon fish sauce
2 teaspoons soy sauce

THAI CURRY PASTE
2 tablespoons chopped lemongrass
  (white part only)
2 tablespoons grated ginger
2 teaspoons grated lime zest
2 teaspoons brown sugar
1 clove garlic, crushed

NOODLE SALAD
4 ounces cellophane or other Asian
  noodles
2 bird's eye or small red chilies, finely
  chopped
¼ cup chopped cashews or peanuts
2-3 stalks cilantro, chopped

Place all the paste ingredients in a mortar and pestle or small food processor (a coffee grinder works well for this) and crush until to a paste. Spread over the lamb fillet, cover, and refrigerate for an hour or overnight.

To make the noodle salad, soak or cook the noodles according to the directions or until softened and tender, swirling with a fork to separate the strands. Drain and rinse well. Place in a bowl and toss with chilies, cashews and cilantro. Whisk together the dressing ingredients and toss through the salad.

Heat a heavy-bottomed or nonstick pan to medium high heat, and add oil. Sear the lamb for 2-3 minutes each side or until cooked as preferred. Take care not to overcook the lamb, as it won't be nearly as tender. Medium rare, or an internal temperature of 120-130° F is ideal. Cover loosely with foil and allow to rest for 10 minutes before slicing thinly and serving tossed with the noodle salad.

A thoroughly decadent twist on a classic Niçoise salad– excellent with a mouth-filling Shiraz! A few tips to making this a real winner– keep the egg yolks moist and soft, the vegetables crisp and tender and don't overcook the duck!

warm duck niçoise

Serves 4 as a light meal or lunch

2 duck breasts, skin and sinew removed
salt and pepper to taste
1 tablespoon olive oil
¾ pound green beans, lightly blanched
12 fingerling potatoes, halved and boiled
    until tender
⅓ cup Niçoise olives
2 hard boiled eggs, quartered

DRESSING
2 tablespoons olive oil
1 tablespoon the Little Penguin Shiraz
1 tablespoon red wine vinegar
2 teaspoons Dijon mustard

Heat a non-stick pan over a medium heat and add the oil. Season the duck breasts with salt and pepper then sauté for 5-6 minutes each side or until cooked as desired. I prefer it still just a little pink inside. Cover with foil and allow to rest for 10 minutes before slicing. The duck can also be chilled to serve as a cold salad.

Place the beans, potatoes and olives in a bowl. Whisk together the dressing ingredients and reserve 1 tablespoon. Toss the remainder through the salad. To serve, slice the duck thickly. Arrange vegetables and eggs on plates or a platter. Top with the duck and drizzle with the remaining dressing.

pinot noir

If fresh peas are out of season, this recipe is also great with frozen peas. They still make for a great soup. But just once, try it with fresh, plump spring peas to experience the freshness and texture. This is also a lovely soup to serve cold.

fresh pea soup

Serves 2-4

⅓ cup vegetable or chicken broth
2 cups fresh peas
2 mint sprigs
½ cup milk
1 tablespoon red wine vinegar
1 tablespoon medium dry sherry, optional
2 tablespoons plain yogurt or buttermilk
squeeze lemon juice
freshly ground pepper

Bring the stock to the boil, add the peas with a mint sprig and simmer for 20-30 seconds or until tender but still bright green. Drain, reserving the liquid, and transfer to a blender. Add the milk, vinegar, sherry and a couple of fresh mint leaves to the peas and puree, adding a little of the reserved liquid if necessary to bring to a desired consistency. Return to saucepan and warm. Serve with a drizzle of yogurt, a squeeze of lemon and fresh ground pepper.

There's a certain magic that surrounds fresh, wild salmon and Pinot Noir - the rich, flavorful salmon with it's velvety texture, paired with a supple, generous wine. Adding the Little Penguin Pinot Noir to this recipe heightens the experience.

grilled mustard salmon with red wine sauce

Serves 4

4 fillets fresh salmon, bones removed
1 tablespoon mustard seeds
1 tablespoon freshly ground pepper
1 tablespoon oregano
2-3 tablespoons olive oil
1 cup the Little Penguin Pinot Noir

MASH
4 medium white potatoes, peeled and halved
¼ cup buttermilk or milk
2 tablespoons butter
freshly ground pepper to taste

To make the mash, place potatoes in a large saucepan of cold, salted water and bring to a boil. Reduce heat and simmer until tender. Drain well, add the buttermilk, butter and pepper, and mash until smooth. If too stiff, add a little more buttermilk or milk. Keep warm.

Brush the salmon with a little of the olive oil. Combine the mustard seeds, pepper and oregano and spread on a plate. Press the flesh side of the salmon into the mixture to form a crust. Heat the remaining oil in a pan and cook the salmon for 1-2 minutes on each side. Transfer to a baking dish, cover with foil and keep warm in a very low oven. It will continue to cook, so make sure you take it out of the pan just a little underdone. It should still be a rich pink and moist inside.

Pour the red wine into the same pan and cook until the wine reduces to a thin sauce consistency. Place mounds of mashed potato on plates, rest the salmon on the side and spoon over the red wine reduction.

Even though the prawns are cooked in white wine (which brings them to life), you can still enjoy this dish with the Little Penguin Pinot Noir. Its soft body and roundness is a great match for the fresh summer flavors and the overall simplicity of the dish.

angel hair pasta with prawns, peas & basil

Serves 4-6

12 ounces angel hair pasta or preferred long pasta

2 tablespoons olive oil

1 cup fresh or frozen peas

½ cup white wine, such as the LIttle Penguin Chardonnay or White Shiraz

juice of 1 lemon

1 pound uncooked peeled prawns, about 18-20

8-10 fresh basil leaves, torn

freshly ground pepper to taste

Cook the pasta according to directions, drain well and place in a large bowl. Toss with a tablespoon of the oil and set aside.

Bring a sauce pan of salted water to boil, add peas and cook for 20-30 seconds. Drain and plunge into a bowl of iced water to stop them cooking further. Drain well and add to the pasta.

Heat the remaining oil in a large fry pan add prawns. Cook, stirring for one minute, then add the wine and lemon juice. Bring to a simmer and cook just until the prawns are bright and opaque. Add the pasta, peas and basil and toss over heat until just heated through. Season to taste with pepper and serve with a loaf of rustic bread.

Simple, elegant and decadent tasting, yet delightfully light and even quite healthy (remember the red wine and dark chocolate theory) - almost too good to be true! So you absolutely must finish it with a scoop of whipped cream or ice cream.

chocolate, date & walnut torte

Serves 4

¼ cup plain flour
1 cup loosely packed dates, chopped
  (look for plump moist ones)
1 ¼ cups walnuts, roughly chopped
½ cup chopped dark cooking chocolate
5 egg whites
1 cup sugar

Preheat oven to 350°F. Lightly grease, flour and line the base of an 8-9 inch cake pan. Place the flour, dates and walnuts in a food processor and pulse on and off until the mixture is a coarse even crumb. Add the chocolate and pulse just to break the pieces up slightly. Tip mixture into a large bowl.

In a separate bowl, beat the egg whites with electric mixers until soft peaks form. Gradually add the sugar, beating until mixture is thick and glossy. Lightly fold the egg whites through the flour mixture until all the dry ingredients are just moistened. Take care not to over-mix or the eggs will lose their volume. Spoon into prepared pan and bake for 25-30 minutes or until cake springs back when gently pressed with your finger. Allow to cool in tin for 5-10 minutes before turning on to a wire rack to cool completely. Store in a sealed container in a cool place until ready to serve.

Just for fun! The bananas may take you by surprise, but they make a deliciously sweet, creamy topping. Similar to ice cream, but better!

frozen mocha martinis

Makes 4

2 cups strong espresso coffee,
   sweetened to taste and frozen in ice
   cube trays

¼ cup half and half

3-4 tablespoons irish cream liquor or
   coffee liquor, or to taste

2 frozen bananas

½ cup crème fraiche or whipped cream

4 chocolate truffles

This drink needs to come together quickly and just before serving, so have all your ingredients and glasses ready - you may even want to chill the glasses in the freezer. Place the frozen coffee cubes in a blender and add the cream. Blend until smooth but still frozen. Divide mixture between the glasses. If the mixture is too liquid place glasses in the freezer for 10-15 minutes before proceeding.

Place the frozen bananas and crème fraiche in a food processor or cleaned blender and puree to a smooth cream. Spoon over the espresso. Thread chocolate truffles onto stirrers and serve immediately with the truffle perched on top of the glass.

cabernet sauvignon

61

corn & wild rice fritters with grilled tomato

When pairing food with Cabernet, most would lean towards rich meat dishes, comfort food and bold flavors. But these fritters, with the deep nutty flavor of the wild rice and the earthy character brought out by grilling the sweet corn, make the Little Penguin Cabernet an ideal pairing.

Makes 6 fritters

GRILLED TOMATOES
6 large cherry tomatoes, halved
1 teaspoon sugar
salt and pepper to taste
To serve, watercress or mache leaves

FRITTERS
olive oil, for cooking
2 green onions, chopped
kernels cut from 2 ears corn
1 cup cooked wild rice or wild rice blend

FRITTERS (cont.)
2 tablespoons finely sliced basil
1 tablespoon snipped chives
2 eggs, whisked
2 egg whites, whisked
salt and freshly ground pepper to taste

To grill the tomatoes, sprinkle the cut sides with sugar, salt and pepper. Heat a non-stick pan and add tomatoes cut side down. Cook for a minute or just until the sugar has caramelized. Transfer to a plate with cut sides up and keep warm in a very low oven.

To make the fritters, heat a large non-stick fry pan over a medium-high heat and add a few teaspoons of oil. Add the green onion and corn kernels and cook, shaking the pan, for 1-2 minutes or until aromatic. Remove from pan and place in a large bowl. Add rice, basil, chives, eggs and egg whites to the corn mixture and mix well. Season to taste.

Wipe out the pan with a paper towel and heat a little more oil. Place 2 or 3 half-cup mounds of the mixture in the pan, leaving room for spreading between each fritter. Gently spread each fritter out to flatten. Cook for 2 minutes or until browned on the underside. Carefully flip over and cook until mixture is just set and browned. Place on absorbent paper and keep warm with the tomatoes while you cook the remainder. Serve fritters topped with tomato and mache or watercress.

Where would a food and wine book be without a deeply rich, saucy beef dish– especially one that only takes minutes to prepare. Choose something to soak up those delicious, meaty juices like polenta or sweet mashed squash. A loaf of chewy Italian bread could do the job quite nicely too.

seared beef with port & mushroom sauce

Serves 4

4 fillet steaks (try New York, filet or sirloin)
2 tablespoons olive oil
1 tablespoon crushed peppercorns

PORT AND MUSHROOM SAUCE
1½ cups sliced mushrooms, try oyster, shitake, crimini or a mixture
2 tablespoons seasoned flour
1 tablespoon olive oil
1 shallot, finely chopped

PORT AND MUSHROOM SAUCE (cont.)
1 leek, cleaned and white part sliced
2 tablespoons tomato paste
1 teaspoon Worcestershire sauce
½ cup beef stock
½ cup port or Cabernet Sauvignon wine
1 tablespoon balsamic vinegar

To make the sauce, toss the mushrooms and flour together in a plastic bag and set aside. Heat olive oil in a large fry pan. Add shallot and leek and cook, stirring for 1-2 minutes or until soft. Add tomato paste and Worcestershire sauce and cook for 1 minute, or until aromatic and the paste has turned a rust color. Add stock, port and vinegar and bring mixture to the boil. Reduce heat, add the mushrooms and simmer, stirring occasionally, until mushrooms are soft and mixture is thickened.

While the mushrooms are cooking, brush steaks with half the oil and coat with the pepper. Heat the remaining oil in a cast iron or non-stick pan and add the steaks. Sear for 2-3 minutes each side for medium rare, or as preferred. Add to the mushroom sauce, and cook over a low heat for 1-2 minutes to allow flavors to infuse, spooning the sauce over the meat as it heats.

cabernet garlic lamb rack with cous-cous

Israeli cous cous, sometimes called 'Pearl' cous cous, has larger grains than regular cous cous and a delightful smooth, luxurious feel - perfect for nestling the lamb and its rich red wine jus.

Serves 4-6

2 Frenched racks of lamb

MARINADE
1 ½ cups the Little Penguin Cabernet Sauvignon
3 tablespoons honey, softened
3 cloves garlic, crushed

ISRAELI COUS COUS
1 tablespoon olive oil
1 green onion, sliced
1 cup Israeli or pearl cous-cous
1 cup white wine or water
1 cup chicken stock
8 dates, seeded and sliced

ISRAELI COUS COUS (cont.)
¼ cup roasted slivered almonds
8 fresh basil leaves, torn
½ red pepper, finely diced
grated zest and juice of ½ orange

Place the racks of lamb in a non-reactive dish, or zip-lock bag. Combine the marinade ingredients. Pour over the lamb, cover and marinate for 2-3 hours or overnight.

To make the cous cous, heat the olive oil in a large saucepan and sauté the green onion for 2 minutes or until softened. Add the cous cous and cook, stirring for 20-30 seconds. Add the wine and chicken stock and bring to the boil. Reduce heat and simmer for 10 minutes or until grains are tender and liquid is absorbed. Transfer to a bowl and fluff with a fork. Add the remaining ingredients and toss well.

Remove the meat from the marinade. Place the marinade in a pan and bring to the boil. Reduce heat and simmer until liquid is starting to thicken to a glaze. Heat a grill to medium high and cook the lamb racks for 5-6 minutes each side for medium rare or as desired. Cover and allow to rest for 5 minutes. Slice the lamb, drizzle with the glaze and serve with the cous cous.

There are few desserts more warm and simply sexy than pears cooked in red wine. Using the Little Penguin Cabernet adds lush berries and soft tannins, and the mascarpone just finishes out all that wonderful flavor and sweetness. Take time to truly enjoy this one– and the aromas it exudes.

wine & honey poached pears with mascarpone

Serves 4

1 ½ cups red wine
½-¾ cup honey, to taste
½ cup cranberry or grape juice
1 stick cinnamon
1 teaspoon peppercorns
4 pears, peeled, cored and quartered
4 tablespoons mascarpone cheese

Combine the wine, honey, juice, cinnamon and peppercorns in a saucepan and bring to a boil. Reduce heat, add the pears and simmer for 10 -15 minutes or until tender. Remove the pears with a slotted spoon and set aside. Continue to cook the wine for 15-20 minutes or until a light syrup. Strain and return to the pan with the pears. Cook over a low heat until the pears are just heated through. Spoon onto plates and top with a dollop of the mascarpone.

pistachio & almond amaretti

Makes about 24 biscuits

½ cup pistachio nuts
¾ cup ground or diced almonds
½ cup self-raising flour
3 egg whites
¾ cup ultra-fine baking sugar
2 teaspoons honey, softened
1 tablespoon finely grated orange zest

Preheat oven to 325°F. Grease or line 2 oven trays. Place the nuts and flour in a food processor (or try a coffee grinder) and process to a coarse crumb. Pour mixture into a large bowl. In a separate bowl beat the egg whites until soft peaks form. While beating, gradually add the sugar and honey and beat until mixture is thick and glossy. Using a large metal spoon, gently fold in the flour and nut mixture with the orange zest. Place teaspoonfuls on lined trays and bake for 12-15 minutes or until pale golden. Transfer to wire racks to cool completely before storing in airtight containers.

The Italians have a lot to teach us in living the good life—enjoyment of good food and wine, and taking the time to do so. These Amaretti are a perfect example. Simple, nutty, sweet, (healthy even) - something to sit down with and linger over while sipping a delicious espresso or red wine.

the Little Penguin

www.thelittlepenguin.com